Welcome	2
1 My birthday	8
2 At school	18
3 My family	28
4 My body	38
5 Pets	48
6 My house	58
7 Food	68
8 I'm happy!	78
Goodbye	88
Festivals	92
Extra practice	96
Picture dictionary	104

1 ✏️ Match and trace.

a) Hello. I'm Beth.

b) Hello. I'm Cody.

c) Hello. My name's Waldo.

d) Hello. My name's Harry.

2   Lesson 1

2 ✏️ 🖍️ Trace. Then colour.

1. blue   2. red   3. yellow   4. green

3 🎧 🖍️ Listen and ✓. Then colour.

1. ☐ yellow ✓ blue

2. ☐ red ☐ green

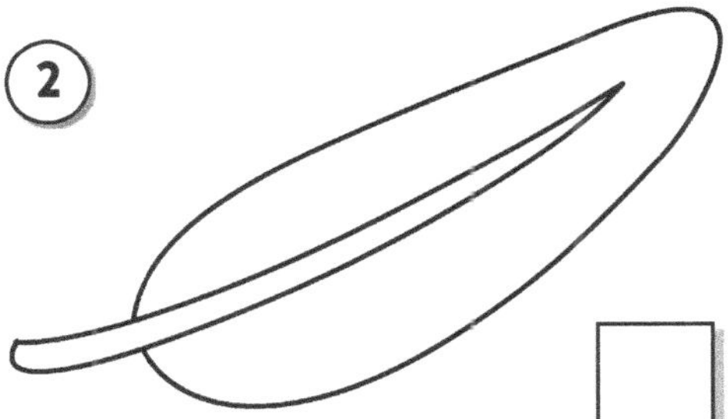

3. ☐ yellow ☐ red

4. ☐ green ☐ blue

Lesson 2

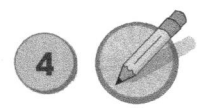 **Read and trace.**

a) 1 — one
b) 2 — two
c) 3 — three
d) 4 — four
e) 5 — five
f) 6 — six
g) 7 — seven
h) 8 — eight
i) 9 — nine
j) 10 — ten

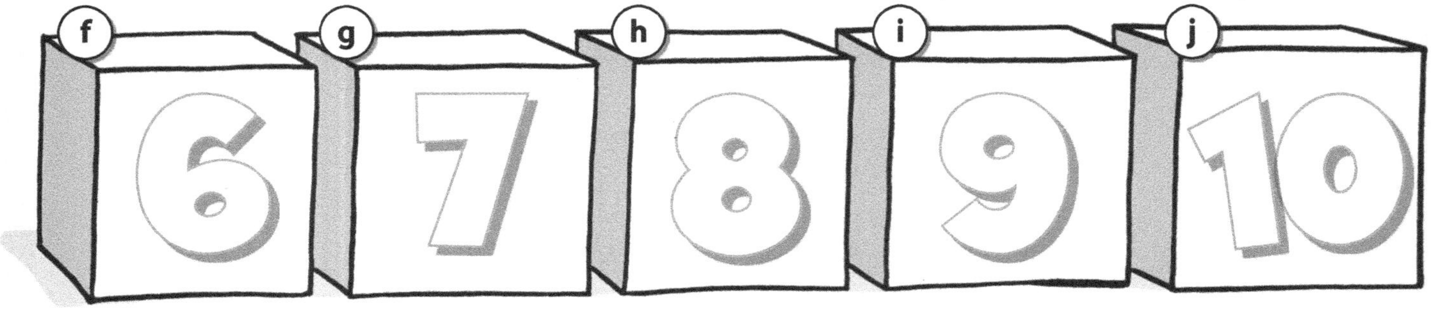

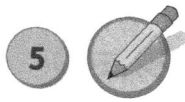 **Count and trace.**

a) one / two
b) four / five
c) eight / nine
d) three / four
e) six / seven

Lesson 3

6 ✏️✏️ **Colour. Then match and trace.**

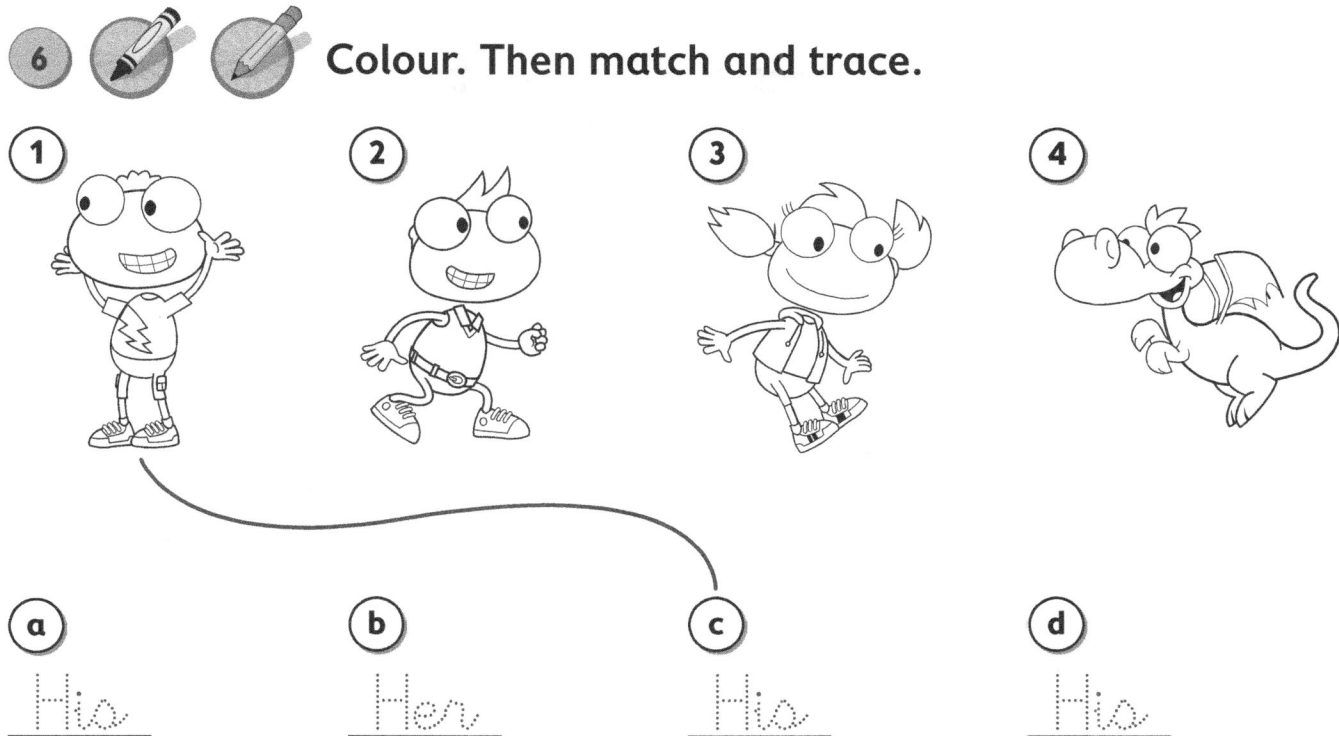

a. His name's Waldo.
b. Her name's Beth.
c. His name's Cody.
d. His name's Harry.

7 ✏️✏️ **Circle and colour.**

1. (His / Her) balloon is blue.
2. (His / Her) balloon is red.

Lesson 4

5

8 🎧 ✏️ Read. Then listen and number.

a ☐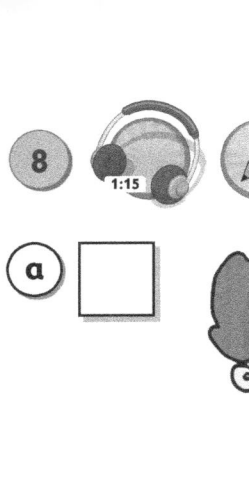
count

b ☐ 1
sit down

c ☐
stand up

d ☐
listen

e ☐
open your book

f ☐
close your book

g ☐
look

h ☐
wave goodbye

Lesson 5

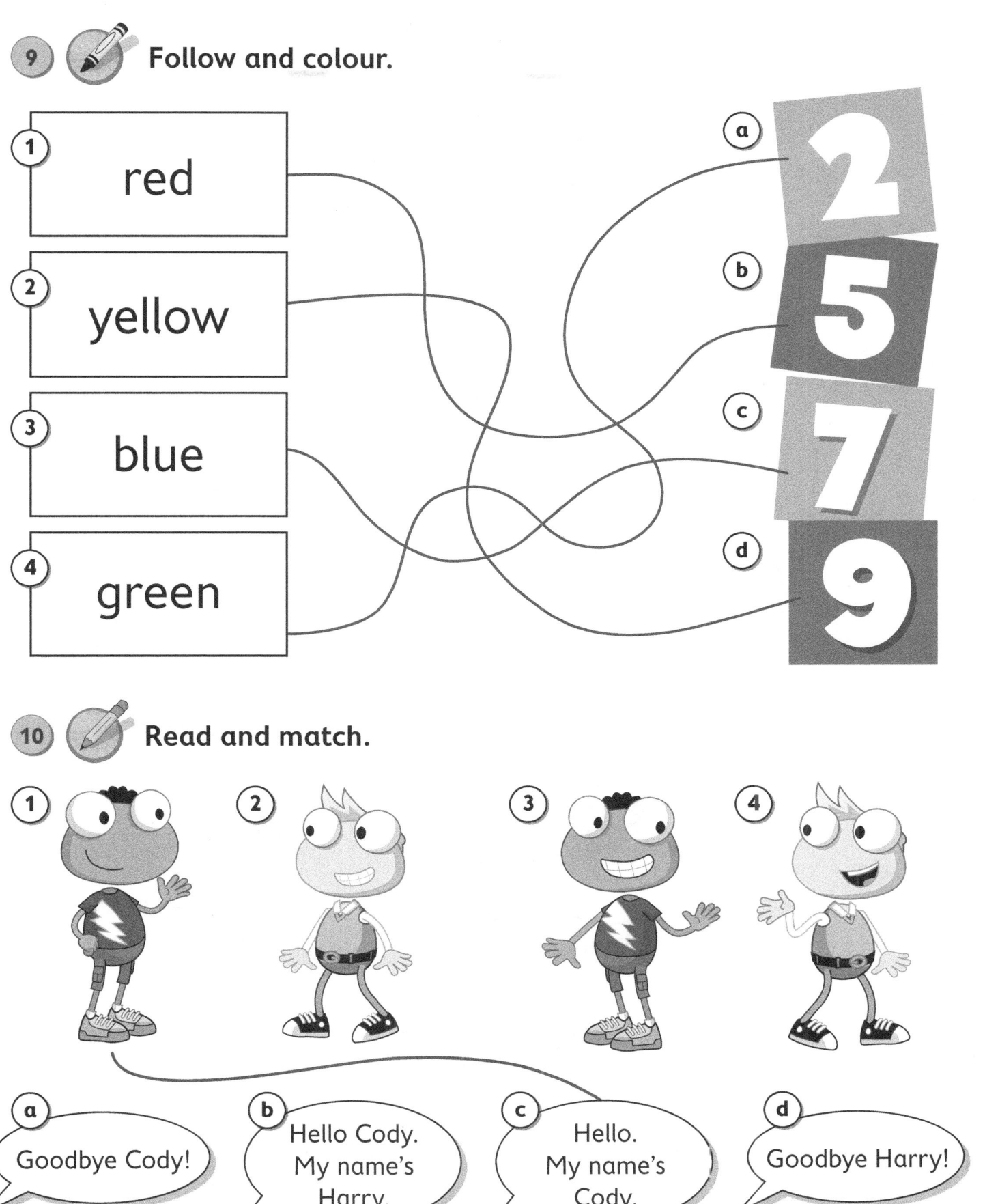

1 My birthday

1 🖉🖉 Trace and colour.

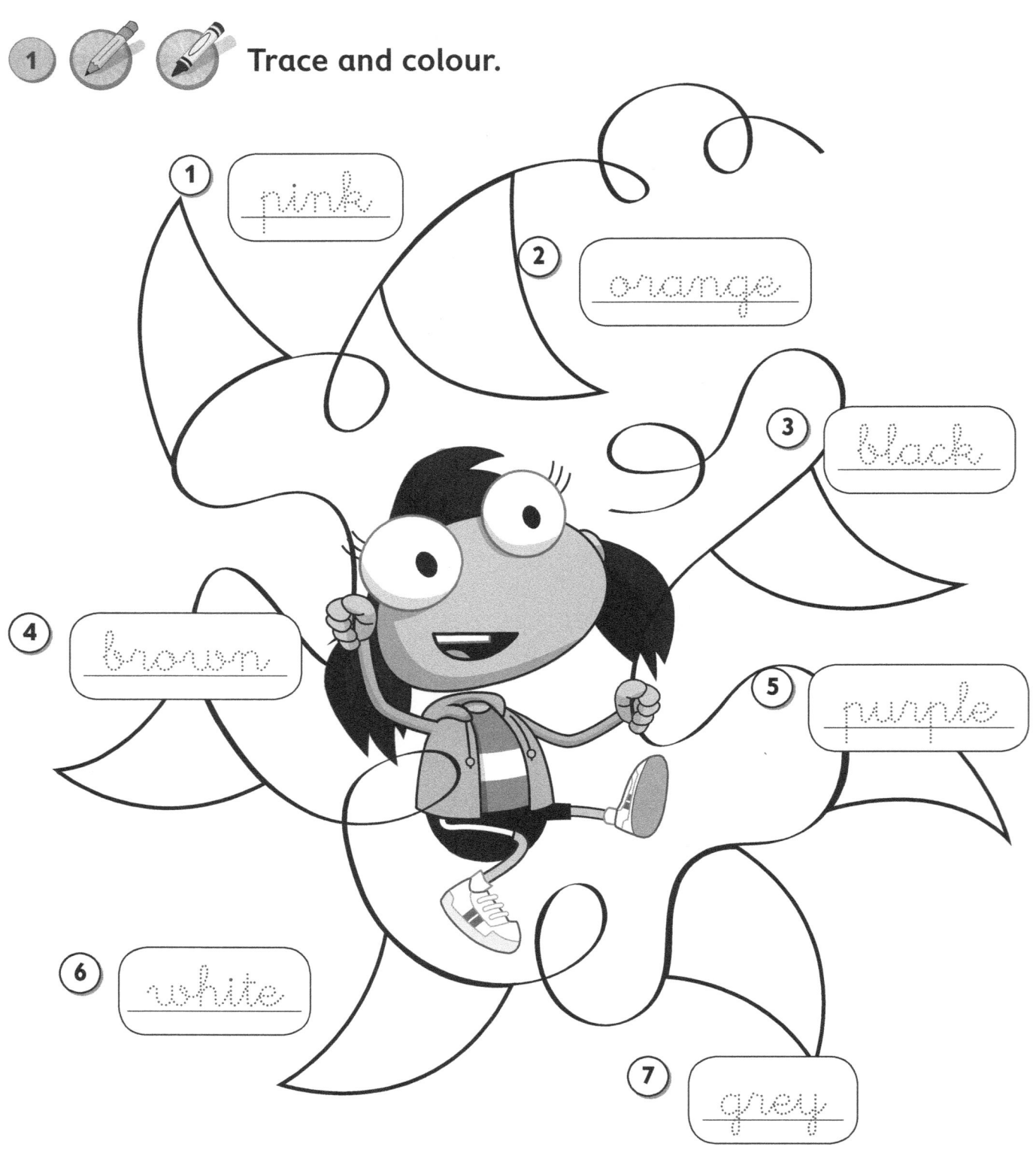

1. pink
2. orange
3. black
4. brown
5. purple
6. white
7. grey

2. Listen and number.

a. ☐ b. Ben ☐ c. Ann [1]

3. Look and trace. Then colour.

a. I'm _four_. My favourite colour is _orange_.

b. I'm _seven_. My favourite colour is _grey_.

c. I'm _nine_. My favourite colour is _pink_.

d. I'm _ten_. My favourite colour is _purple_.

Lesson 2

4  Match. Then trace.

1 	a 	stamp
2 	b 	climb
3 	c 	run
4 	d 	jump
5 	e 	dance
6 	f 	clap
7 	g 	hop
8 	h 	walk

5  **Read and trace. Then colour.**

1

What colour is it?

It's ___purple___.

2

What colour is it?

It's ___orange___.

3

What colour ___is it___?

It's blue.

4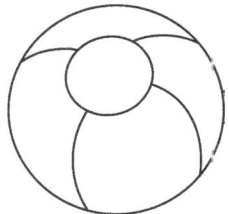

What colour is it?

___It's___ yellow.

5

Is it red?

___No___, it isn't. It's pink.

6

Is it brown?

___Yes___, it is.

7

Is it white?

No, ___it isn't___. It's green.

8

Is it black?

Yes, ___it is___.

Lesson 4

  Listen and circle. Then colour.

1   2

3

  Look and ✓ or ✗.

1    2

Lesson 5

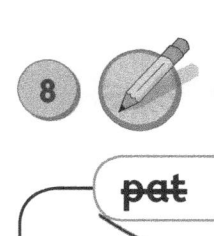

8 Read the words and circle.

~~pat~~   tap

9 Listen to the sounds and circle the letters.

1   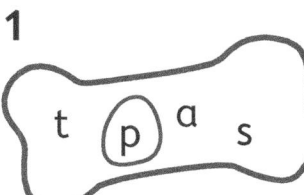   t (p) a s

2   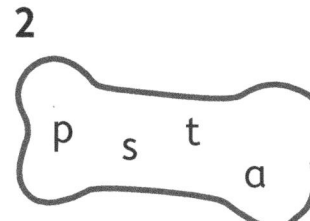   p s t a

3   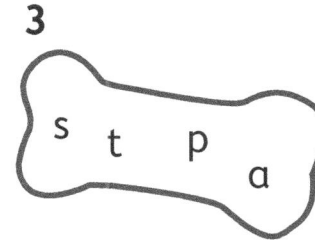   s t p a

4   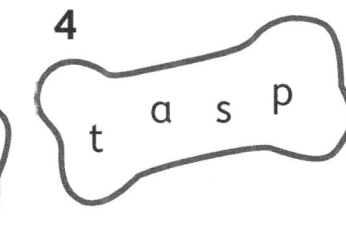   t a s p

10 Listen and write the letters.   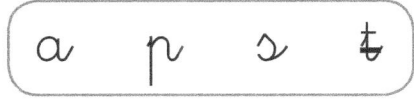 a p s t

1 t   2 ____   3 ____   4 ____

11 Listen and circle the words.

1 (sat) / at   2 tap / pat   3 at / pat   4 pat / sat

Lesson 6

13

12 Match. Then trace.

1. flower
2. bird (foot)
3. bird
4. butterfly
5. leaf

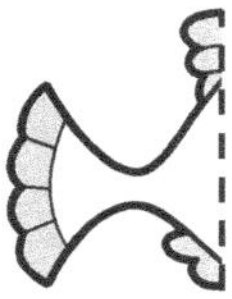

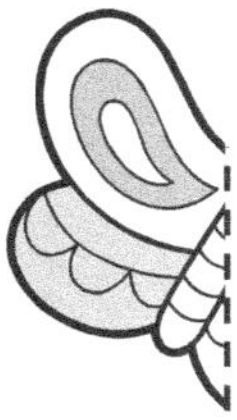

a. butterfly
b. bird
c. leaf
d. flower
e. fish

flower
butterfly
leaf
fish
bird

13 Colour. Then circle.

1. fish   leaf   bird

2. flower   butterfly   bird

Lesson 7

Wider World

14 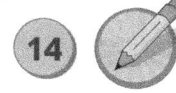 Trace and match.

1. birthday cake
2. balloon
3. present

a

b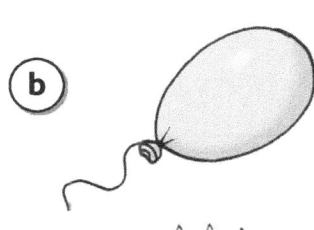

c

15 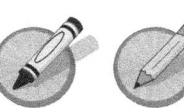 Draw and colour. Then write.

1. How old are you? _____.
2. How many balloons? _____.
3. What colour is the present? _____.

Lesson 8

16  **Read and colour.**

1	black
2	brown
3	blue
4	purple
5	pink
6	orange
7	green
8	grey

17 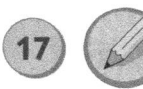 **Look and circle.**

1 What's your name? (My name's Harry.) / His name's Cody.

2 How old are you? It's six. / I'm six.

3 What's your favourite colour? My favourite colour is blue. / His favourite colour is blue.

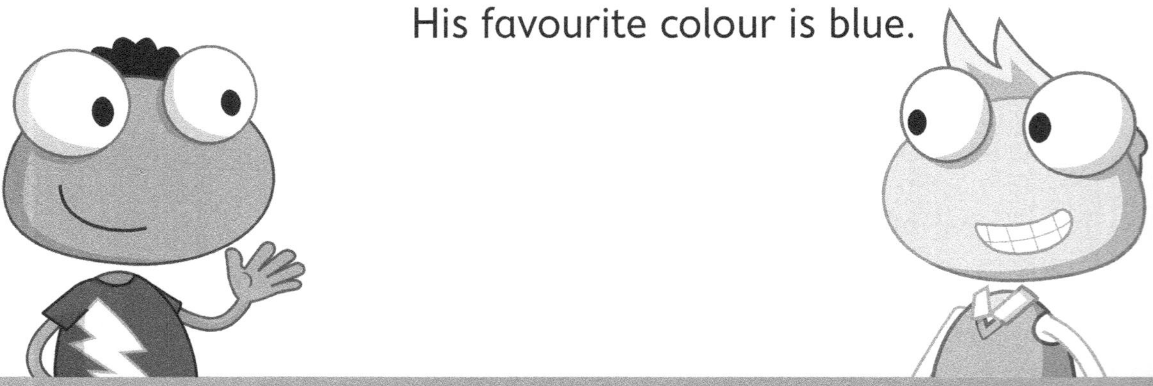

18   **Read and trace. Then colour.**

Hello. **¹** My name's Ana.

² I'm seven.

My favourite colour **³** is pink.

Look! A **⁴** pink butterfly!

Goodbye!

19    **Draw and write.**

Hello. My name's _____.

I'm _____.

My favourite colour is _____.

Goodbye!

2 At school

1 Draw. Then trace.

1. rubber
2. pen
3. pencil
4. pencil sharpener
5. pencil case
6. ruler
7. book
8. table
9. chair
10. desk

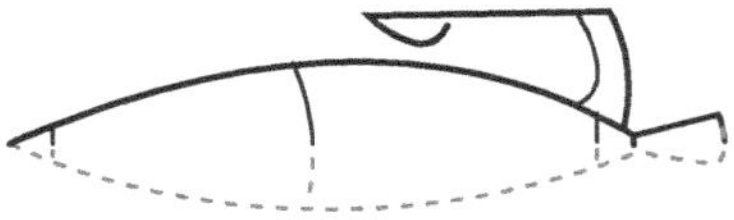

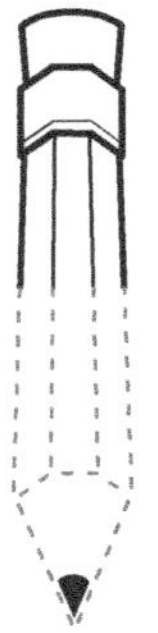

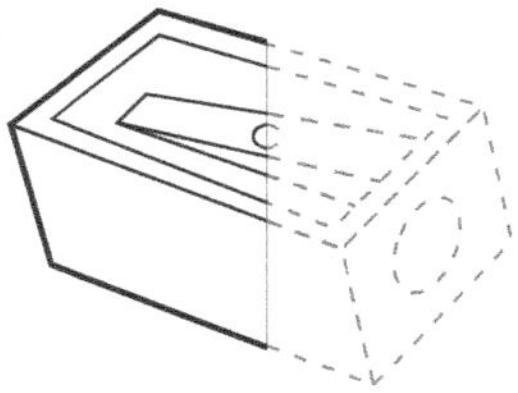

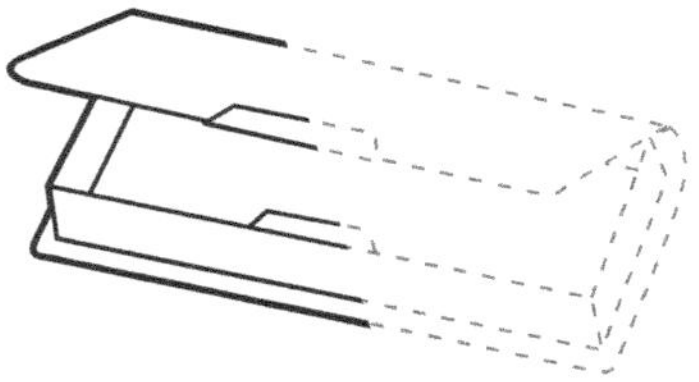

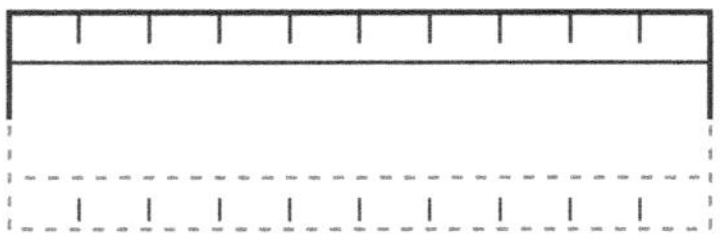

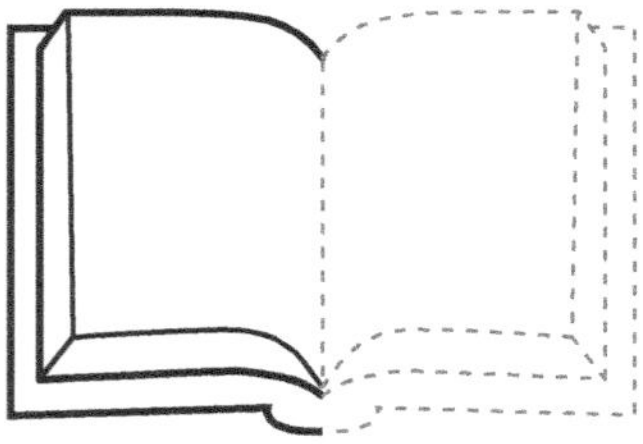

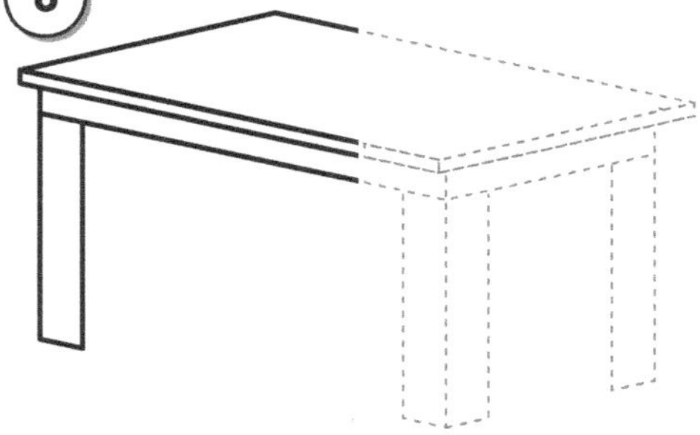

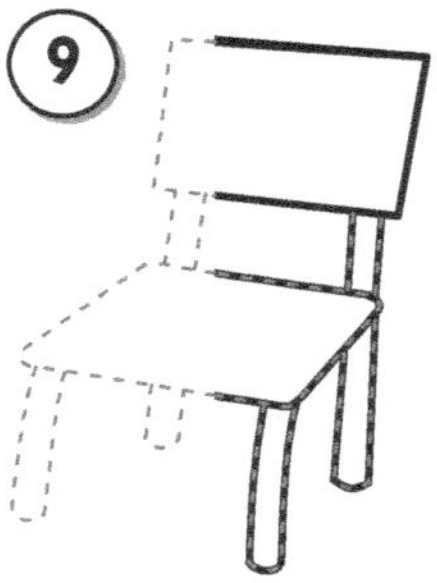

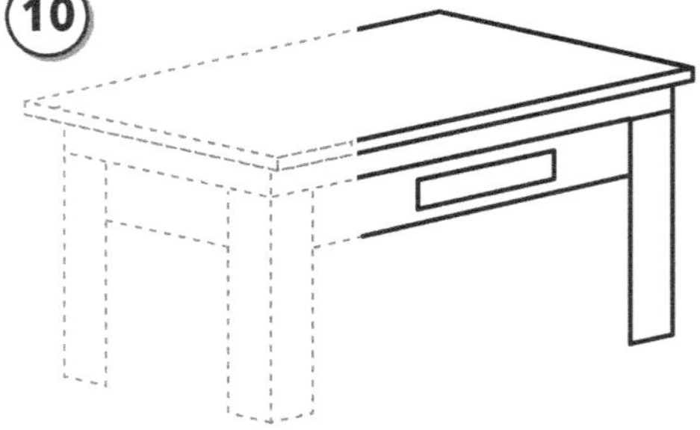

Lesson 1

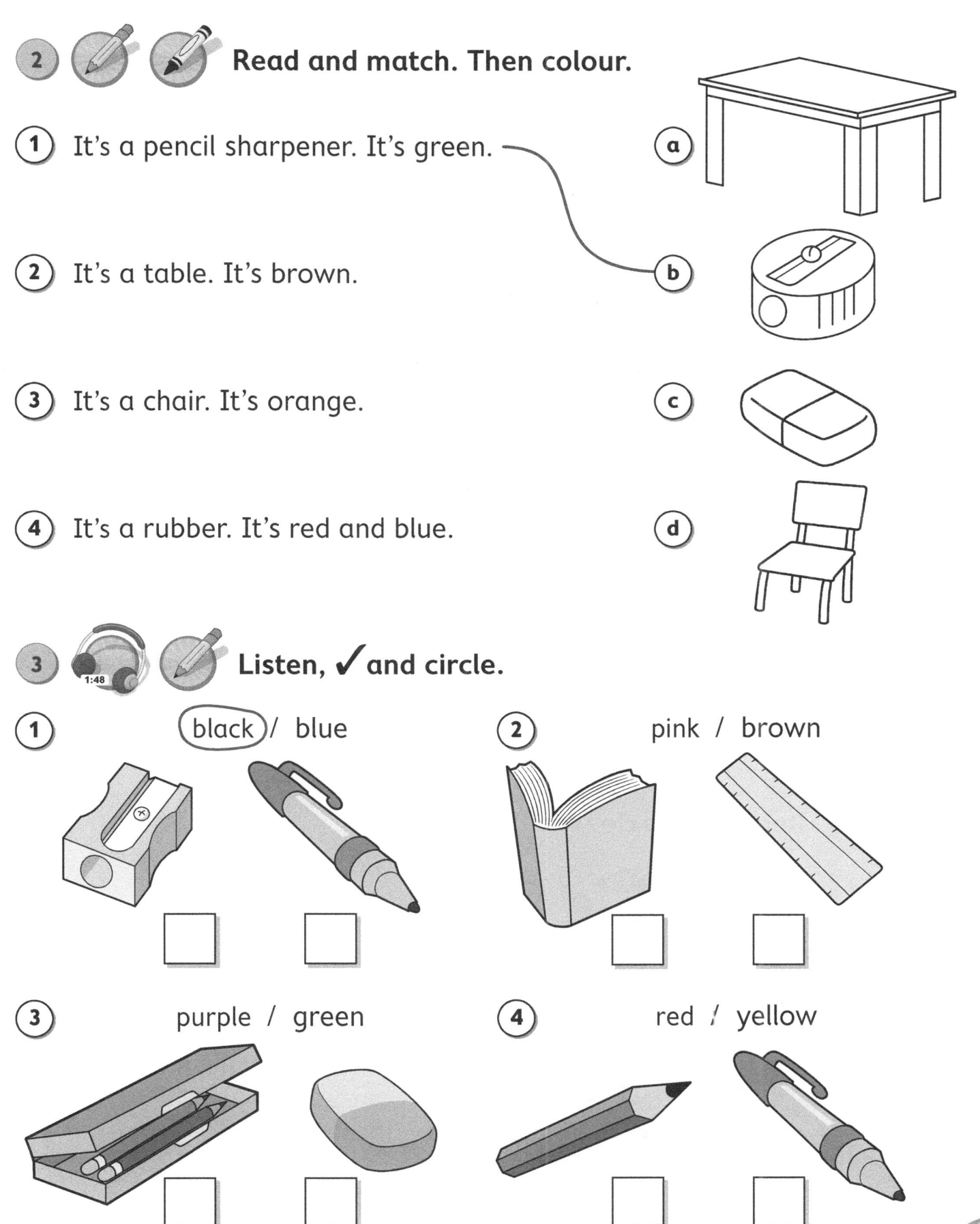

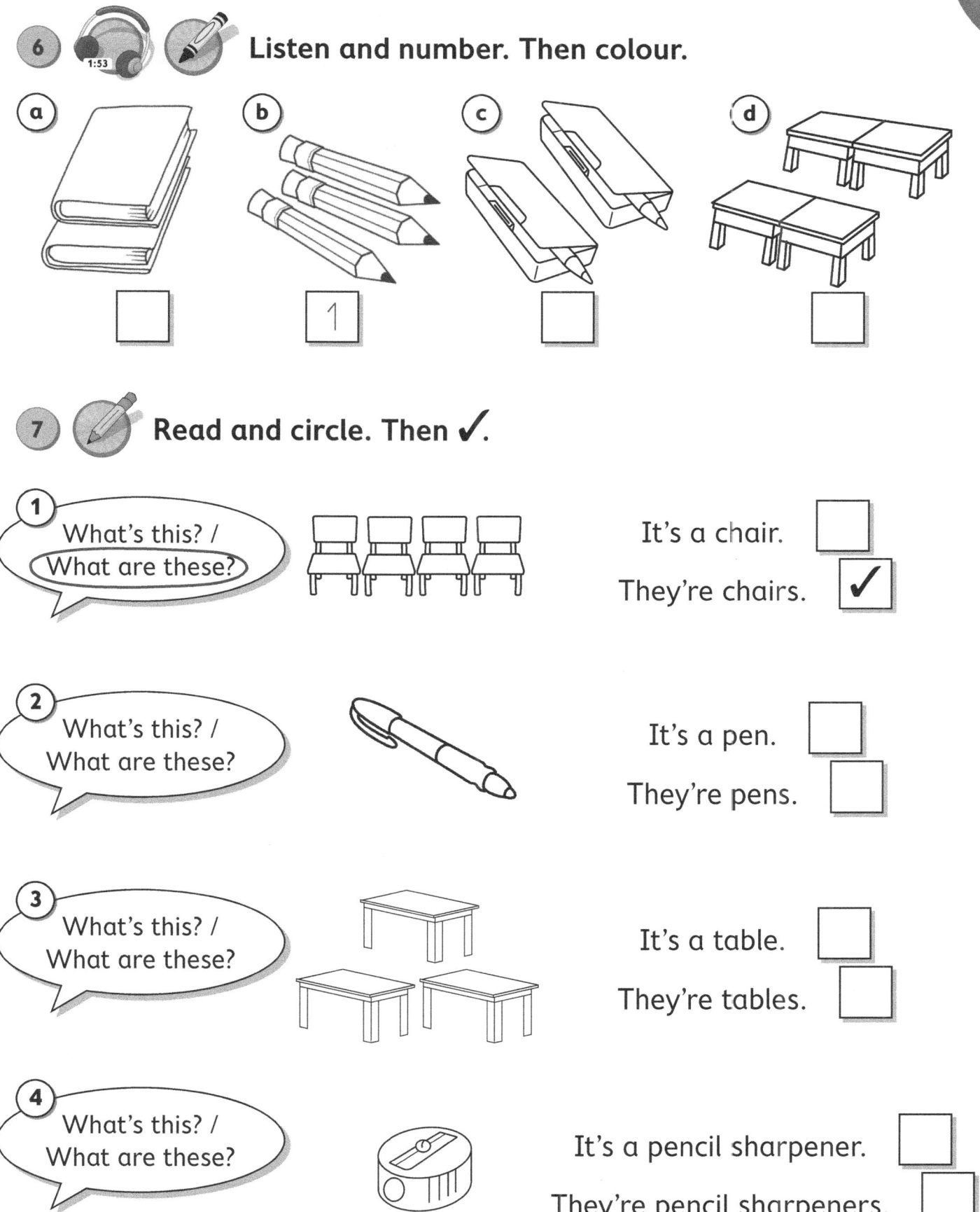

  Listen and number. Then colour.

  Draw. Then circle and colour.

What's this?

It's a green (rubber / dragon).

  Look and ✓ or ✗ what you do at school.

22   Lesson 5

11 Read the words and circle.

~~dip~~   man   nap   pan

PHONICS
d   i   m   n

12 Listen to the sounds and circle the letters.

1. a, ⓓ, m, n
2. d, m, i, p
3. a, i, n, t
4. p, d, i, t

13 Listen and write the letters.   d   i   ~~m~~   n

1. _m_   2. ____   3. ____   4. ____

14 Listen and circle the words.

1. (sit) / dip   2. dad / am   3. dip / man   4. it / sit

Lesson 6

15 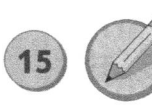 Match and trace.

1 2  3  4

a  b  c  d

piano   _guitar_   _drum_   _violin_

16  Read and circle.

1 2 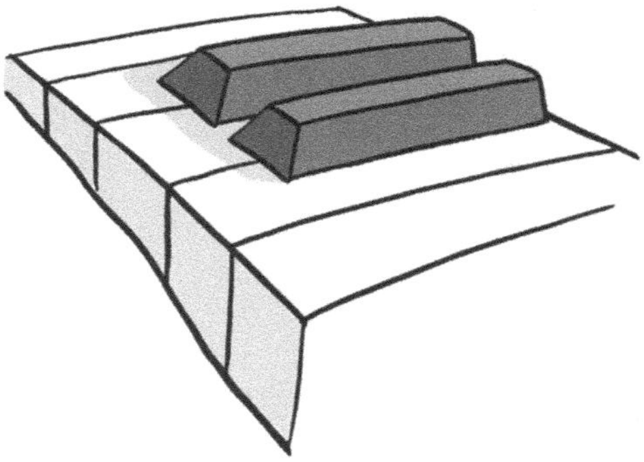 3

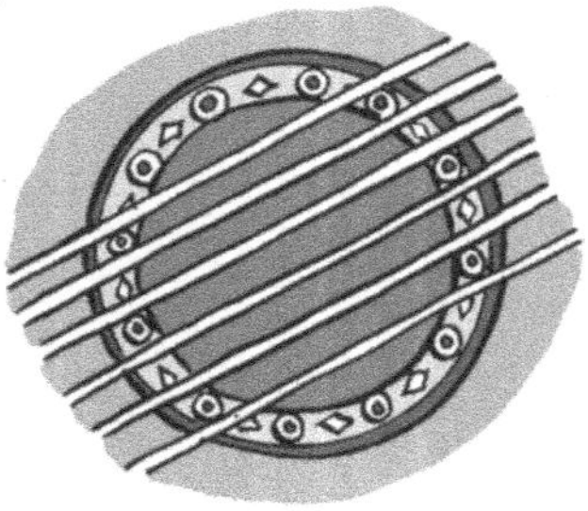

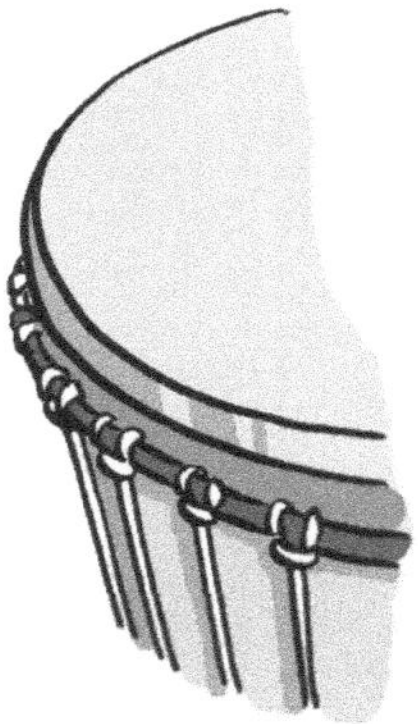

It's a ((guitar) / drum).   It's a (piano / violin).   It's a (piano / drum).

24 Lesson 7

Wider World

17 Trace and match.

1. school
2. playground
3. teacher
4. pupil

a
b
c
d

18 Look, count and trace.

1 How many tables can you see?   two / three
2 How many chairs can you see?   five / six
3 How many pencils can you see?   one / three

Lesson 8

19   Read and match. Then colour.

a red ruler

a green book

a yellow rubber

a pink pencil

a blue pencil case

an orange pencil sharpener

a black chair

a brown table

a purple pen

20  Join the dots. Then read and circle.

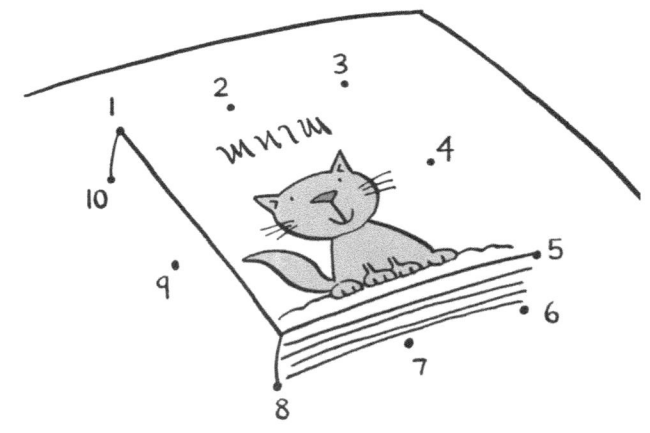

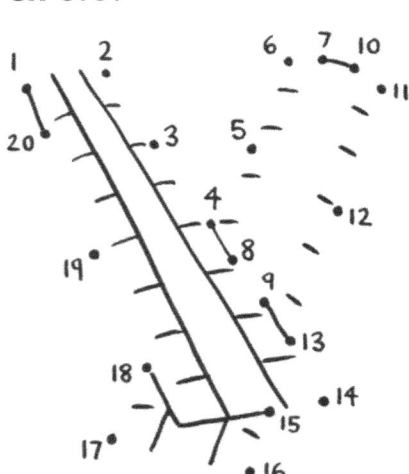

(What's this?) / What are these?

It's a book. / They're books.

What's this? / What are these?

It's a ruler. / They're rulers.

26 Lesson 9

21  **Read and circle. Then colour.**

¹ (**This** / These) is my desk.

² (This / **These**) are my books. They're red and blue.

And ³ (**this** / these) is my pencil case. It's pink.

Can you see two pens?

They're green.

22   **Draw your desk and write.**

This is my _____.

These are my _____.

They're _____.

And this is my _____.

It's _____.

Can you see _____?

They're _____.

Lesson 10

3 My family

1 ✏️ Trace and number.

① mum ② dad ③ sister ④ brother

This is my *family*.

⑤ grandad
⑥ granny
⑦ friend

Lesson 1

2   Find and colour. Then read and circle.

This is my (mum /(friend)).   This is my (granny / sister).
((He's)/ She's) ((nine)/ ten).   (He's / She's) (seven / eight).

3 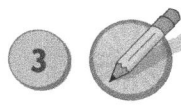 Trace and match.

1 How old is he? __He's eight__ .

2 How old is she? __She's seven__ .

3 How old is she? __She's five__ .

4 How old is he? __He's ten__ .

Lesson 2

29

4  Look and write.

vet   pilot   doctor   dentist
~~cook~~   artist   farmer   dancer

cook

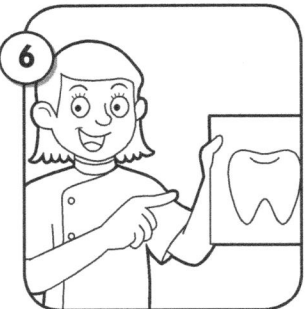

5  Read and circle.

 My (mum / dad) is a (farmer / doctor).

 My (mum / dad) is a (pilot / teacher).

6  **Match. Then read and circle.**

1 Is she a doctor? (Yes, she is. / No, she isn't.)
2 Is she an artist? (Yes, she is. / No, she isn't.)
3 Is he a vet? (Yes, he is. / No, he isn't.)
4 Is he a teacher? (Yes, he is. / No, he isn't.)

7   **Listen and ✓. Then write.**

~~cook~~ doctor
artist pilot

1  ☐ Yes, he is.
✓ No, he isn't.
He's a ___cook___.

2  ☐ Yes, she is.
☐ No, she isn't.
She's a _____.

3  ☐ Yes, he is.
☐ No, he isn't.
He's an _____.

4  ☐ Yes, she is.
☐ No, she isn't.
She's a _____.

Lesson 4

10 Read the words and circle.

~~can~~   cap   dig   dog

PHONICS
c g o

11 Listen to the sounds and circle the letters.

1. g c t **o**
2. c o g a
3. i g a p
4. o a c g

12 Listen and write the letters. c g o

1. c   2. ___   3. ___

13 Listen and write the words.

1. g a o   2. ___ ___ ___   3. ___ ___ ___   4. ___ ___ ___

Lesson 6

14  **Read and write.**

1. It's a *painting*.
2. It's a _____.
3. It's a _____.
4. It's a _____.

15   **Colour and circle.**

1 = red   2 = yellow   3 = orange   4 = green   5 = brown

It's a (drawing / sculpture). It's a (bird / butterfly).

34 Lesson 7

16   Look and draw. Then listen and number.

17  Complete for you. Then ask a classmate.

	me	classmate
How old are you?		
What's your mum's name?		
What's your brother's / sister's / friend's name?		
How old is your brother / sister / friend?		

Lesson 8

  **Listen. Circle *True* or *False*.**

1 (True) / False
2 True / False
3 True / False
4 True / False
5 True / False

 **Look at Activity 18. Read and circle.**

1. This is my ((mum) / dad). She's a (vet / (pilot)).

2. This is my (dad / grandad). He's a (doctor / farmer).

3. This is my (sister / brother). (His / Her) name's Rita.

4. This is my (sister / brother). (He's / She's) four.

5. This is (Amy / Rita). (He's / She's) my friend.

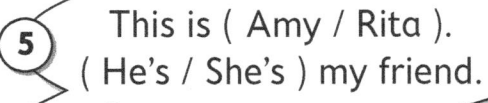

 **20 Read and write.**

mum ~~dad~~ brother

This is my family. This is my
¹ __dad__ . He's a doctor.
His name's Paul.

My ² _____ is a vet.
Her name's Alice.

And this is my ³ _____.
He's two! His name's Sam.

   **21 Draw one person in your family and write.**

This is my
_____.

He's / She's a
_____.

His / Her name's
_____.

Lesson 10

4 My body

1 🖊 **Look and write.**

~~head~~ feet leg hand body fingers arm

1. head
2. ___
3. ___
4. ___
5. ___
6. ___
7. ___

Lesson 1

2 Read. Then circle.

	a	b	c
1 foot			
2 wings			
3 hand			
4 arms		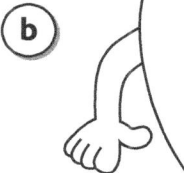	

3 Listen and circle. Then colour.

1 I've got a (pink / purple) body.

2 I've got (brown / orange) hands.

3 I've got (yellow / blue) feet.

Lesson 2

39

  **Read and match. Then write and colour.**

socks   skirt   T-shirt   hat
dress   jumper   trousers   ~~shoes~~

  1. I've got brown shoes.    a 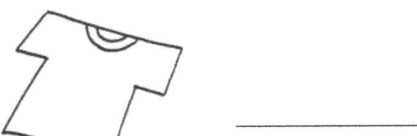 _____

  2. I've got a pink hat.   b  _____

  3. I've got a red dress.   c  _____

 4. I've got purple socks.   d  *shoes*

 5. I've got a green jumper.    e  _____

 6. I've got black trousers.    f _____

 7. I've got a blue skirt.   g  _____

 8. I've got a grey T-shirt.   h  _____

Lesson 3

5  **Count and write. Then colour.**

one   six   four   eight   ~~one~~

1 She's got __one__ head. It's red.
2 She's got _____ arms. They're black.
3 She's got _____ feet. They're blue.
4 She's got _____ toes. They're yellow.
5 She's got _____ body. It's green.

6 **Follow. Then choose and write.**

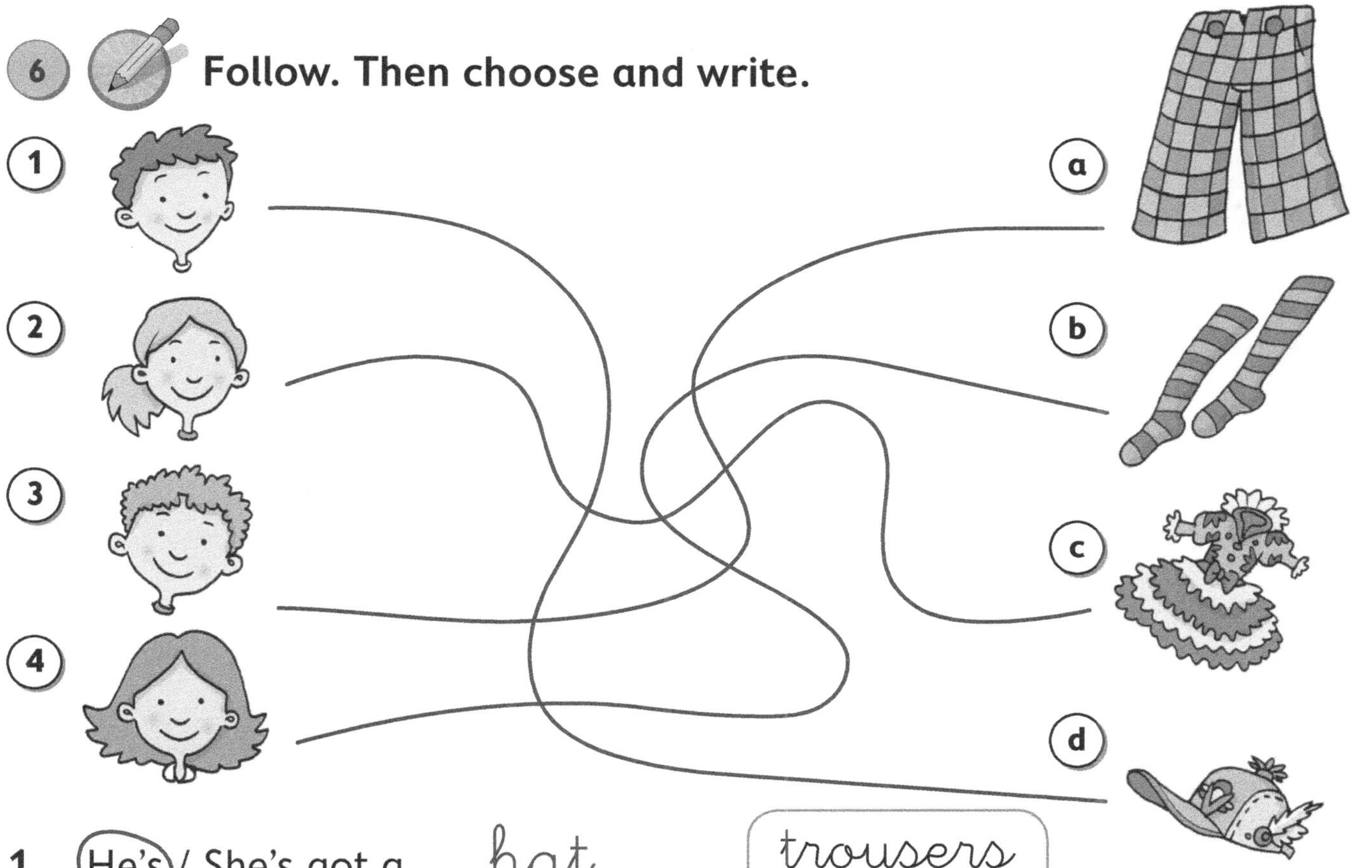

1 a
2 b
3 c
4 d

1 (He's) / She's got a __hat__.
2 He's / She's got a _____.
3 He's / She's got _____.
4 He's / She's got _____.

trousers
dress
~~hat~~
socks

Lesson 4

  **7** Draw. Then ✓ or ✗ and write correct sentences.

four   two   four

1 I've got five heads. ☐

I've got _____ heads.

2 I've got three arms. ☐

I've got _____ arms.

3 I've got two legs. ☐

I've got _____ legs.

 **8** Look and ✓ = clean or ✗ = not clean.

1

2

9  Read the words and circle.

~~kick~~   kid   neck   sock

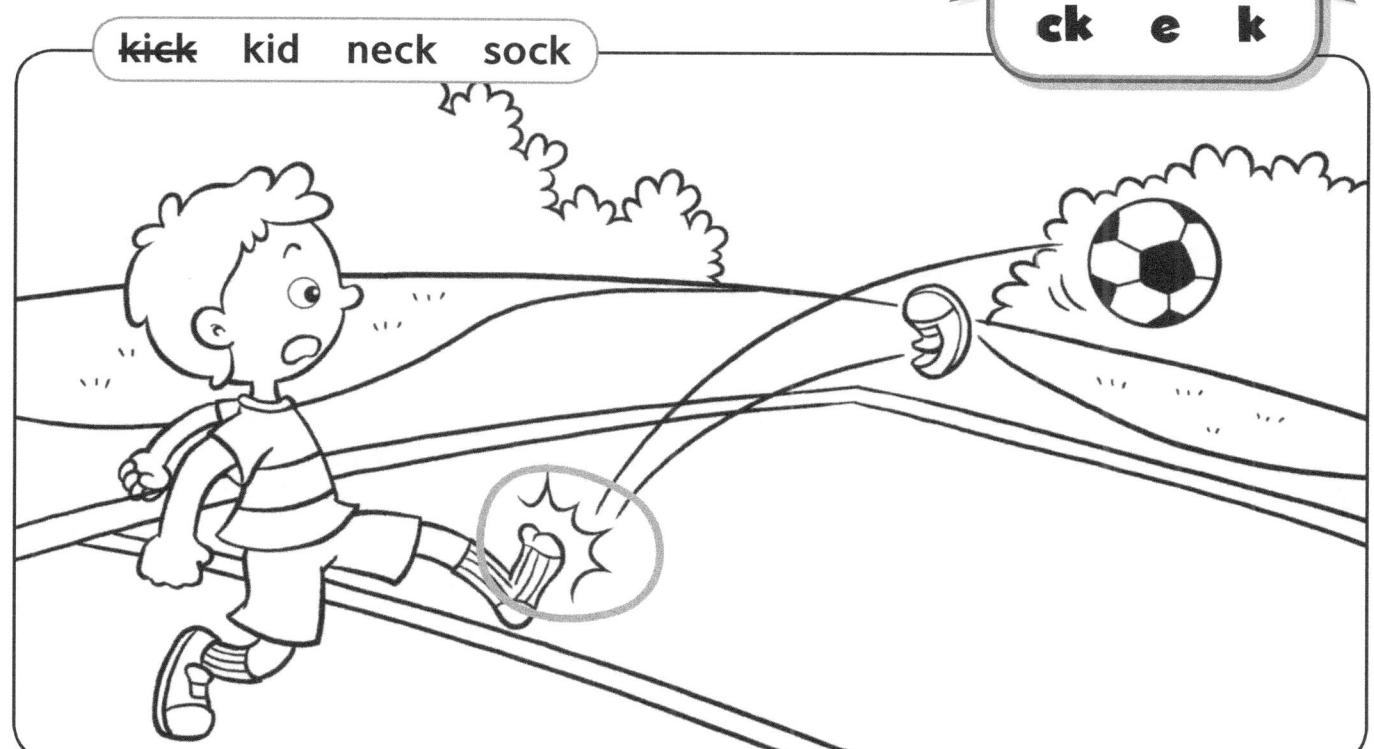

10   Listen to the sounds and circle the letters.

1 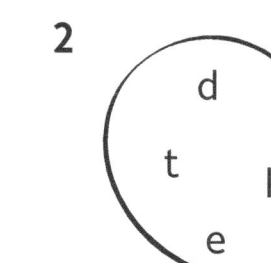   2 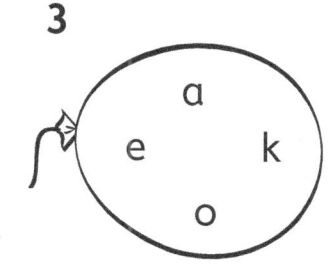   3   4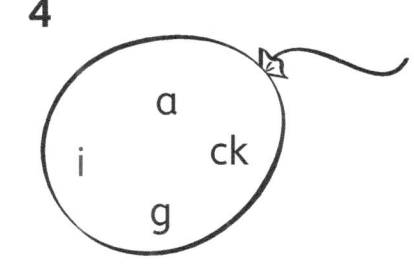

11  Listen and write the letters.

1 _k_   2 _____   3 _____

12 Listen and write the words.

1 _k i t_   2 _____   3 _____   4 _____

Lesson 6

43

13  **Read and circle.**

1. I've got dirty ((hands) / feet).
2. I've got (dirty / clean) feet.
3. Wash your (hands / feet).
4. Wash your (hands / feet).
5. I've got (dirty / clean) hands.
6. I've got clean (hands / feet).

14  **Listen and check your answers.**

Lesson 7

Wider World

15 Read and match.

a) I'm a bird.

b) I'm a butterfly.

c) I'm a dinosaur.

16 Choose a carnival costume. Colour and write.

a dress   wings
a mask   a hat
trousers
a T-shirt

This is my carnival costume.

I've got _____ and _____.

Lesson 8

17   **Read and circle. Then colour.**

1 I've got a (body / (foot)).
((It's)/ They're) green.

 a

2 I've got three (finger / fingers).
(It's / They're) pink.

 b

3 I've got five (leg / legs).
(It's / They're) brown.

 c

4 I've got (feet / foot).
(It's / They're) orange.

 d

18 **Look and ✓ or ✗.**

1 He's got a clean T-shirt. ✗

2 She's got a dirty dress. ☐

3 He's got dirty shoes. ☐

4 She's got clean shoes. ☐

Lesson 9

19 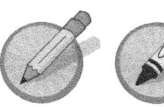 **Read and write. Then colour.**

arms   eight   ~~head~~   three

This is my monster. He's got one ¹ __head__. It's yellow. He's got a green body.

He's got two ² _____. They're pink. And he's got ³ _____ purple fingers.

He's got three legs. They're blue. And he's got ⁴ _____ black feet.

He's got a green hat.

His name's Spike!

20   **Draw a monster and write.**

This is my monster.

He's got one _____.

It's _____.

He's got _____.

They're _____.

He's got _____.

They're _____ His name's _____!

Lesson 10

5 Pets

1 ✏️ Look and write.

> frog   cat   dog   hamster   mouse
> ~~parrot~~   rabbit   snake   tortoise

1.
   parrot

2.
   _____

3.
   _____

4.
   _____

5.
   _____

6.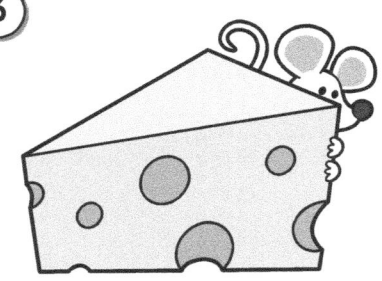
   _____

7.
   _____

8.
   _____

9.
   _____

Lesson 1

2. Find and circle.

① a snake   ② two frogs   ③ a parrot   ④ a tortoise   ⑤ three mice

3. Look at Activity 2. Read and circle.

1 (What's that?) / What are those?   (It's a snake.) / They're snakes.
2 What's that? / What are those?   It's a frog. / They're frogs.
3 What's that? / What are those?   It's a parrot. / They're parrots.
4 What's that? / What are those?   It's a tortoise. / They're tortoises.
5 What's that? / What are those?   It's a mouse. / They're mice.

4 Look and write. | young ~~small~~ thin old tall fat big short |

1 small   2 _____   3 _____   4 _____

5 _____   6 _____   7 _____   8 _____

5 Look and write. | frog ~~rabbit~~ cat dog |

1 He's got a rabbit.   2 She's _____.
3 _____.   4 _____.

Lesson 3

6 🎧 ✏️ **Listen, look and ✓.**

1	Yes, he has.	✓	2 Yes, she has.	☐
	No, he hasn't.	☐	No, she hasn't.	☐
3	Yes, he has.	☐	4 Yes, she has.	☐
	No, he hasn't.	☐	No, she hasn't.	☐
5	Yes, he has.	☐	6 Yes, she has.	☐
	No, he hasn't.	☐	No, she hasn't.	☐

7 ✏️ **Read and circle about your pets.**

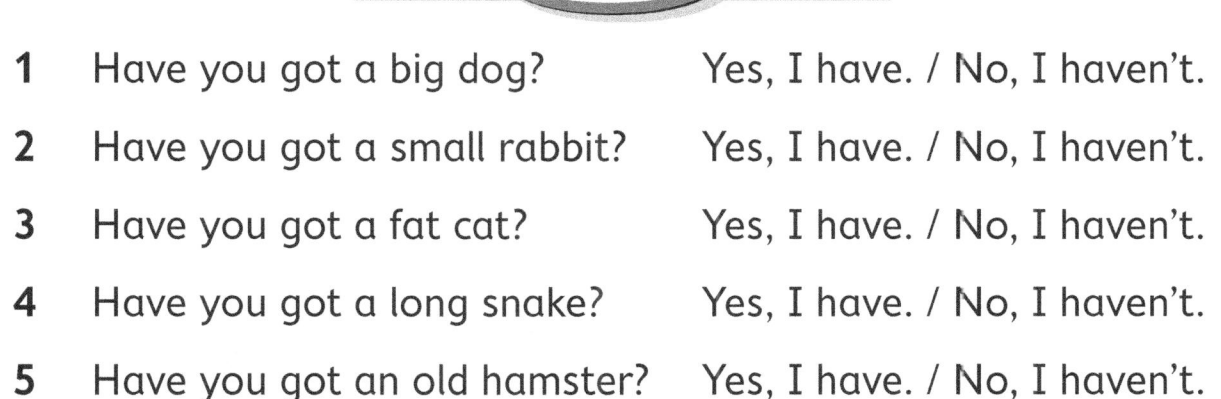

1. Have you got a big dog?   Yes, I have. / No, I haven't.
2. Have you got a small rabbit?   Yes, I have. / No, I haven't.
3. Have you got a fat cat?   Yes, I have. / No, I haven't.
4. Have you got a long snake?   Yes, I have. / No, I haven't.
5. Have you got an old hamster?   Yes, I have. / No, I haven't.

Lesson 4

  **Listen and number.**

 **Who lives here? Look and match.**

52 Lesson 5

10 🖉 Read the words and circle.

~~bag~~ cup hat rat

PHONICS

b h r u

11 🎧 🖉 Listen to the sounds and circle the letters.

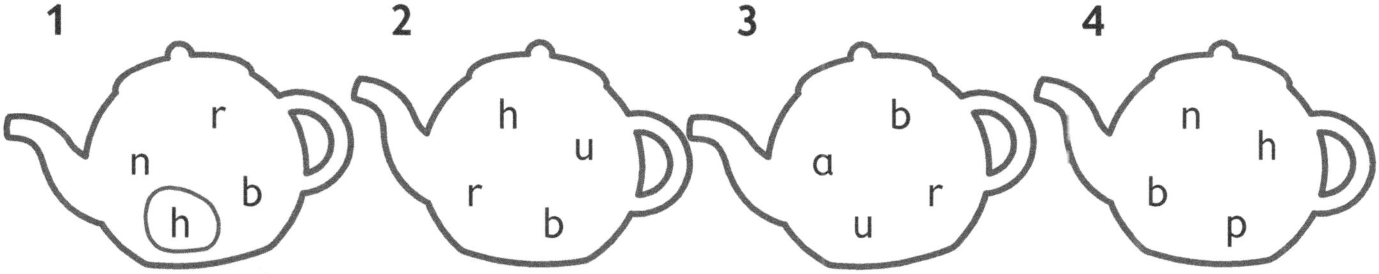

1. (h) n r b
2. h u r b
3. b a r u
4. n h b p

12 🎧 🖉 Listen and write the letters.   b h ~~r~~ u

1. r
2. ___
3. ___
4. ___

13 🎧 🖉 Listen and write the words.

1. u p
2. ___
3. ___
4. ___

Lesson 6

14  **Write. Then match.**

chick   kitten   puppy

1   2   3

_____   _____   _____

15  Join the dots. Then read and circle.

It's a (kitten / puppy / chick).

It's a (kitten / puppy / chick).

Wider World

16 Follow and write.   rat   tortoise   ~~spider~~

1  I've got a _spider_.

2  I've got a _____.

3  I've got a _____.

a b c

17 Look at Activity 16 and write.

Yes, I have
No, I haven't

1  Have you got a snake? _____.

2  Have you got a snake? _____.

18 Read and answer.

1 Have you got an unusual pet? _____.

2 What pet have you got? _____.

Lesson 8

19  **Read and answer.**

~~Yes, he has~~   No, he hasn't
Yes, she has   No, she hasn't

1 Has he got a dog?
   _Yes, he has_____.

2 Has she got a rabbit?
   _____.

3 Has he got a parrot?
   _____.

4 Has she got a frog?
   _____.

20  **Read and match. Then write.**

thin   small   ~~old~~   long   young   ~~fat~~

1 What's that?
   It's a dog. It's __old__ and __fat__.

2 What are those?
   They're snakes. They're _____ and _____.

3 What are those?
   They're kittens. They're _____ and _____.

56 Lesson 9

21 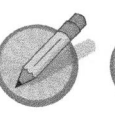  **Read and circle. Then colour.**

I've got a ¹(puppy / (kitten)).

He's ²(small / big) and orange.

He's got ³(two / four) legs.

He's got a ⁴(long / short) tail.

⁵(His / Her) name's Minty.

22   **Draw a pet and write.**

I've got a _____.

He's / She's _____ and

_____.

He's / She's got _____ legs.

He's / She's got a

_____ tail.

His / Her name's _____.

Lesson 10

6 My house

1. Draw. Then write.

bathroom   bedroom   garden   door
kitchen   living room   ~~window~~

1. window

Lesson 1

  **Listen and number. Then read and match.**

She's in the bathroom.
He's in the garden.

They're in the kitchen.
They're in the living room.

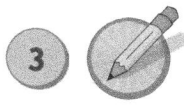 **Join the dots. Then read and circle.**

(Where's / Where are) Waldo?

He's in the (kitchen / living room).

Lesson 2

4  **Listen and number. Then write.**

fridge bath sink
TV sofa bed
cooker lamp

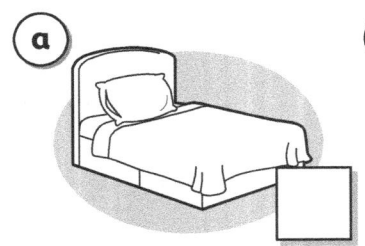 a

 b 1

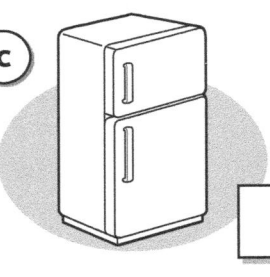 c

 d

 e

 f

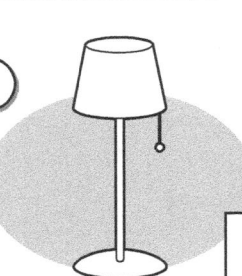 g

 h

5 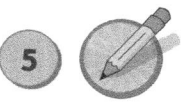 **Look, read and circle.**

1 They're in the (bathroom / bedroom).

2 They're in the (living room / bathroom).

3 They're in the (garden / kitchen).

60 Lesson 3

6  **Read and find. Then circle and write.**

under   in   on

1 (**There's** / There are) a bird ___under___ the window.
2 (There's / There are) two rabbits _____ the fridge.
3 (There's / There are) a teddy _____ the bath.
4 (There's / There are) two dogs _____ the table.
5 (There's / There are) books _____ the bed.
6 (There's / There are) a boy _____ the sofa.
7 (There's / There are) a cat _____ the bed.

Lesson 4

  Listen and ✓ or ✗.

  Look and match.

Lesson 5

9 Read the words and circle.

~~bell~~   doll   fan   leg

10 Listen to the sounds and circle the letters.

1 f / ff / **s** / ll
2 h / o / ff / ll
3 l / h / f / r
4 i / f / t / l

11 Listen and write the letters.

$f \quad ff \quad l \quad ll$

1 ll   2 _____   3 _____   4 _____

12 Listen and write the words.

1 fig   2 _____   3 _____   4 _____

Lesson 6

13  Write. Then listen and follow the path.

café ~~house~~ library playground shop

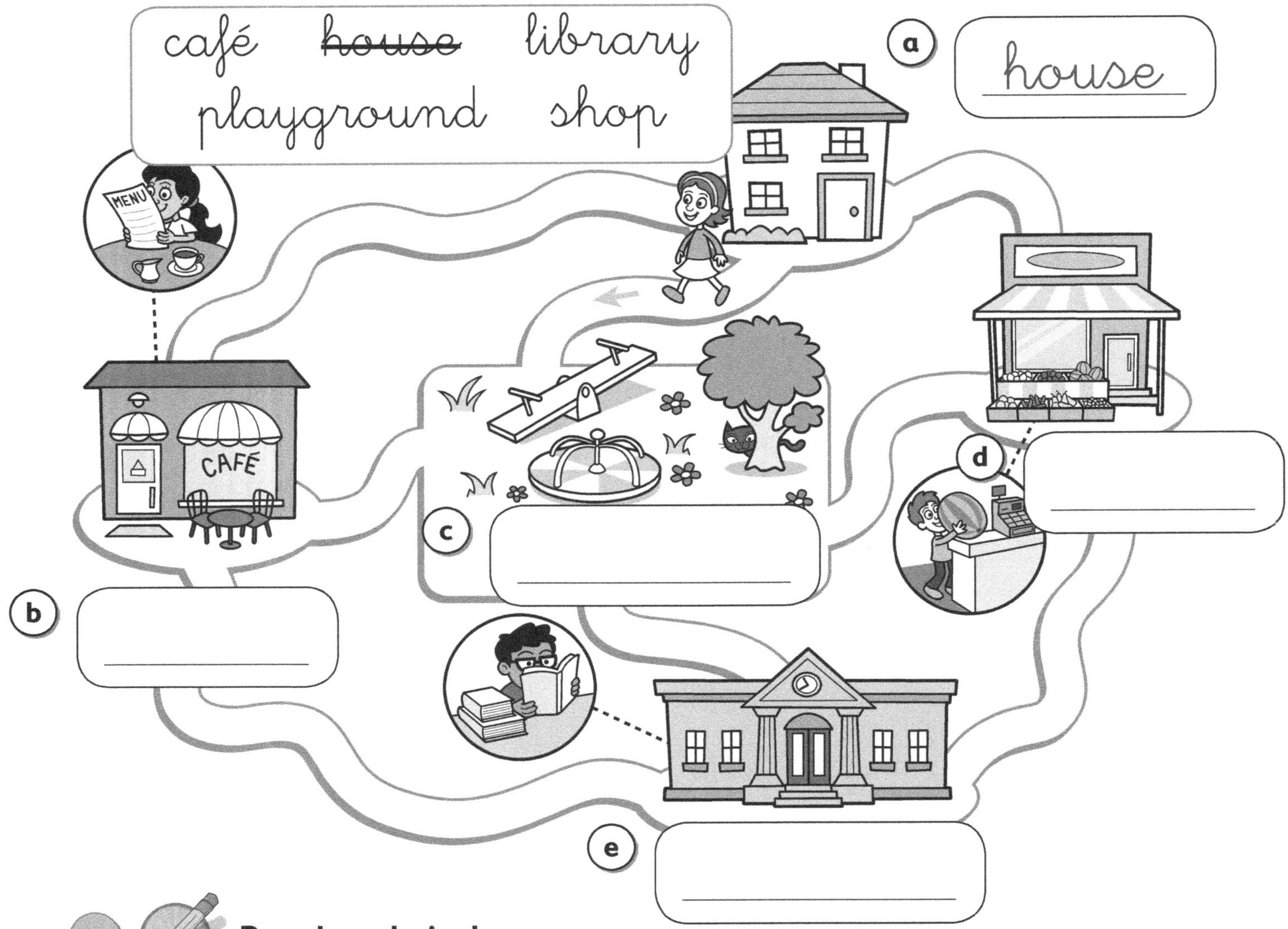

a. house
b. _____
c. _____
d. _____
e. _____

14  Read and circle.

She's in the
(playground / (café)).

It's in the
(shop / park).

He's in the
(library / café).

Lesson 7

Wider World

15 Read and match.

1  — d. house
2  — a. flat
3  — b. caravan
4  — c. houseboat

Word box: cat ~~house~~ bed living room bedroom kitchen TV bedrooms bathroom garden

16 Read and complete the letter.

Hi! My name's Ella.
I live in a small ¹ **house**.
There's a ² _____, a ³ _____,
a ⁴ _____ and two ⁵ _____.
And there's a big ⁶ _____.
My favourite room is my ⁷ _____.
I've got a big ⁸ _____ and a ⁹ _____.
And I've got a ¹⁰ _____! Her name's Cleo.
Goodbye!

Lesson 8

17  **Listen and draw.**

Lesson 9

18  **Read and write.**

lamp ~~bedroom~~ chairs big two

My favourite room is my
¹ __bedroom__.

It's ² _____.

There are ³ _____ beds and two ⁴ _____.

There's a table.

There's a ⁵ _____ on the table.

I've got a TV.

19  **Draw your favourite room and write.**

My favourite room is my _____.

It's _____.

There's _____.

There are _____.

I've got a _____.

Lesson 10

7 Food

1 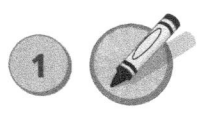  Draw. Then write.

bread   cake   cheese
fish   fruit   milk
salad   yoghurt

1

2

3

4

5

6

7

8

Lesson 1

2   **Find and colour. Then ✓ or ✗.**

I like...

- salad ☐
- fish ☐
- yoghurt ☐
- fruit ☐
- bread ☐
- milk ☐
- cheese ☐
- cake ☐

3  **Read and draw.**

I like fish and salad. I don't like cheese.

I like juice.

Lesson 2

4 ✏️ **Look and number.**

| honey ☐ | ice cream ☐ | water 1 | vegetables ☐ |
| jelly ☐ | chocolate ☐ | sandwich ☐ | meat ☐ |

5 🎧 3:10 ✏️ **Listen and number. Then circle and write.**

1 I ((like) / don't like) __honey__ .
2 I (like / don't like) _____ .
3 _____ .
4 _____ .

cheese
~~honey~~
jelly
meat

Lesson 3

6 🎧 ✏️ Listen and number.

7 ✏️ Look and write.

1. Do you like jelly?
   _____, I _____.

2. Do you like honey?
   _____, I _____.

Lesson 4

10 Read the words and circle.

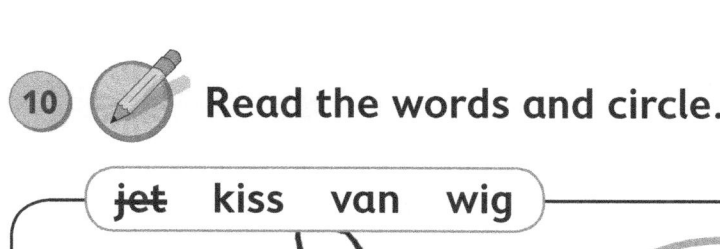

jet kiss van wig

11 Listen to the sounds and circle the letters.

1 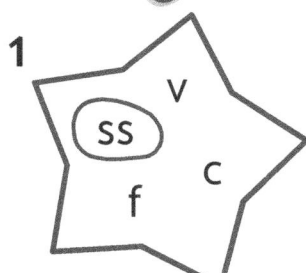   2 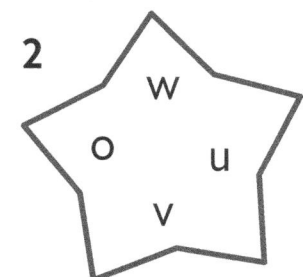   3 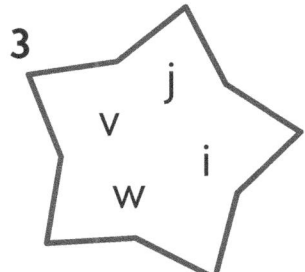   4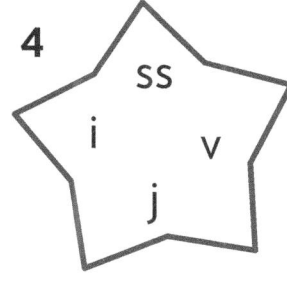

12 Listen and write the letters.

1 _w_   2 _____   3 _____   4 _____

13 Listen and write the words.

1 _mess_   2 _____   3 _____   4 _____

Lesson 6

14 Follow and write.

sausages   chips   carrots

1.
2.
3.

a. _____
b. _____
c. _____

15 Read and ✓. Then draw.

It's good for me!

fruit ☐
salad ☐
cake ☐
bread ☐
yoghurt ☐
milk ☐
juice ☐
chocolate ☐

Wider World

16 What has Ella got? Listen and ✓.

meat	✓	vegetables	☐
fish	☐	salad	☐
fruit	☐	water	☐
ice cream	☐	juice	☐
yoghurt	☐	milk	☐

17 What have you got? Ask a classmate and ✓.

meat	☐	vegetables	☐
fish	☐	salad	☐
fruit	☐	water	☐
ice cream	☐	juice	☐
yoghurt	☐	milk	☐

Lesson 8

18   **Listen, draw and write.**

I like   ~~I don't like~~   I like   I don't like

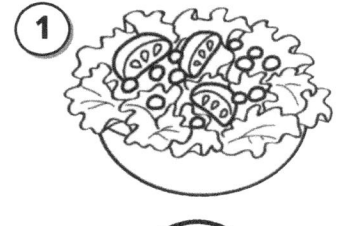 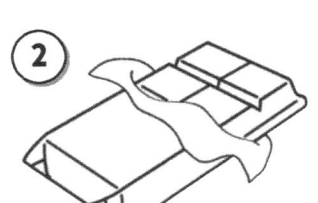  

I don't like salad.

19 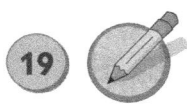 **Read. Then look and write.**   Yes, I do   No, I don't

1. Do you like milk?   Yes, I do.

2. Do you like juice?   _____.

3. Do you like meat?   _____.

Lesson 9

20  **Read and circle.**

I ¹(like / don't like) meat and chips.

I ²(like / don't like) fruit.

My favourite food is ³(pizza / salad).

I ⁴(like / don't like) sausages.

21  **Draw your favourite food and write.**

I like _____ and _____.

I don't like _____.

My favourite food is _____.

Lesson 10

8 I'm happy!

1 ✏️ Look and write.

`happy   hungry   scared   thirsty   tired`

I'm _____.

I'm _____.

I'm _____.

I'm _____.

I'm _____.

Lesson 1

2 🎧 ✏️ Listen and circle.

1. (Yes, I am.) / No, I'm not.
2. Yes, I am. / No, I'm not.
3. Yes, I am. / No, I'm not.
4. Yes, I am. / No, I'm not.

3 ✏️ Find. Then read and circle.

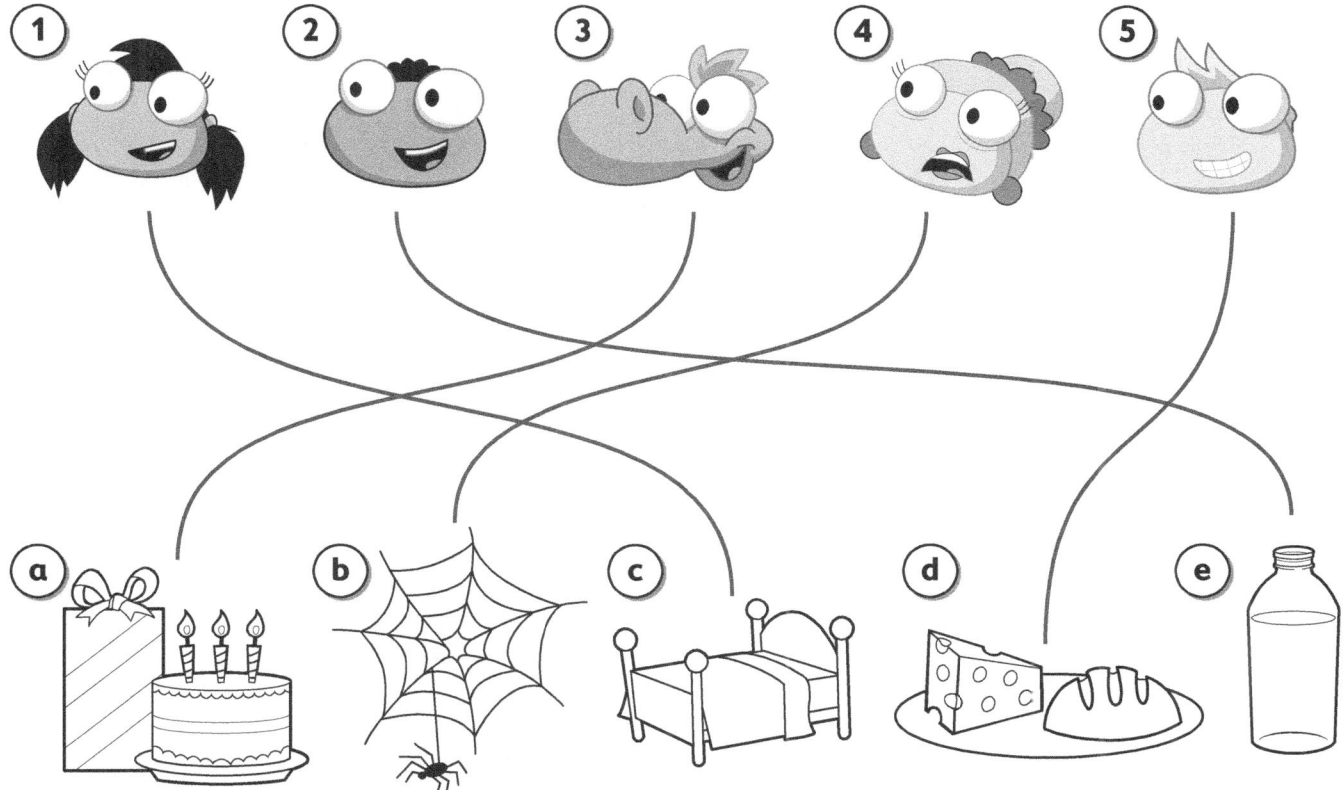

1. She's (happy / tired).
2. He's (thirsty / tired).
3. He's (happy / thirsty).
4. She's (scared / hungry).
5. He's (happy / hungry).

Lesson 2

 **Look and write.**

angry   bored   cold
~~happy~~   hot   hurt
sad   ill

①  ②  ③ 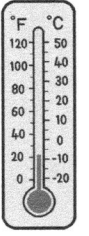 ④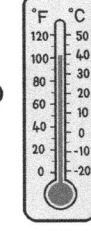

She's _happy_.   He's _____.   She's _____.   He's _____.

⑤  ⑥  ⑦  ⑧

She's _____.   He's _____.   She's _____.   He's _____.

⑤ 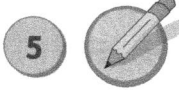 **Read and answer the questions. Then draw yourself.**

Yes, I am   No, I'm not

1 Are you happy?   _____.
2 Are you cold?   _____.
3 Are you angry?   _____.
4 Are you bored?   _____.
5 Are you hungry? _____.

80 Lesson 3

6   **Listen and number.**

7 **Look. Then circle and write.**

① Are you happy?

Yes, I am. / No, I'm not.

I'm _____.

② Are they hot?

Yes, they are. / No, they aren't.

They're _____.

③ Is she bored?

Yes, she is. / No, she isn't.

She's _____.

④ Is he tired?

Yes, he is. / No, he isn't.

He's _____.

Lesson 4

  **Listen and number.**

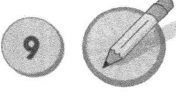 **Look and write.** `hurt   help   sad`

Are you _____ ?   Are you _____ ?   Can I _____ you?

10 Read the words and circle.

~~box~~   buzz   taxi   yes

Phonics

qu   x   y
z   zz

11 Listen to the sounds and circle the letters.

1. z, y, ⓧ, j
2. x, z, y, zz
3. ck, qu, y, zz
4. w, x, qu, ck

12 Listen and write the letters.

qu   x   y   ~~z~~   zz

1. z   2. ____   3. ____   4. ____   5. ____

13 Listen and write the words.

1. quiz   2. _____   3. _____   4. _____

Lesson 6

14  Look and match.

It's hot.

It's cold.

15 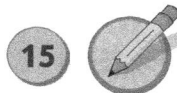 Look and circle.

It's a (polar bear / penguin).

It's (hot / cold).

It's a (turtle / snake).

It's (hot / cold).

16 Read and match. Then circle.

a I'm Anna. I live in Florida. It's (hot / cold) here. I like the (sea / snow).

b My name is Ben. I live in Alaska. It's (hot / cold) here. I like the (sea / snow).

17 What about you? Draw and write.

My name is _____.

I live in _____.

It's _____ here.

I like the _____.

Lesson 8

 **Write.** angry bored cold hot hungry hurt ill thirsty

1.

Are you _____?

Yes, I am.

2.

Is he _____?

Yes, he is.

3.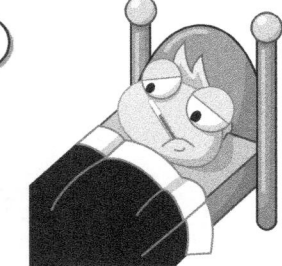

Is he bored?

No, he isn't.

He's _____.

4.

Is she _____?

Yes, she is.

5.

Is he _____?

Yes, he is.

6.

Are you hot?

No, I'm not.

I'm _____.

7.

Is she _____?

Yes, she is.

8.

Is he cold?

No, he isn't.

He's _____.

19   **Read and circle. Then colour.**

This is me on my birthday.

I'm ¹(happy / sad).

I've got ²(three / five) balloons.

They're red, green and blue.

And I'm ³(hungry / thirsty).

I've got a ⁴(big / small) chocolate cake!

20   **Draw yourself on your birthday and write.**

This is me on my birthday.

I'm _____.

I've got _____ balloons.

They're _____.

I'm _____.

I've got a _____ birthday cake!

Lesson 10

Goodbye

1 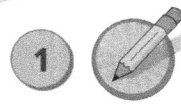 Look and write.

apple   balloon   bird   cake   door
hat   photo   tablet   teddy

1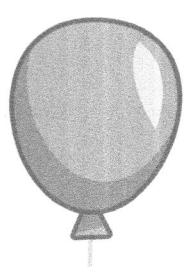

2

3

4

5

6

7

8

9

Lesson 1

2  Listen and number.

3 Look and write.

1.
We like _____.

2.
I've got two _____.

3.
This is my pet. It's a _____.

4.
Do you like _____? Yes, I do.

Lesson 2

89

4 Look, circle and write.

1 Is it a cat?
(Yes / No), it _____.

2 Is it a pencil?
(Yes / No), it _____.

3 Is it a head?
(Yes / No), it _____.

4 Is it a cake?
(Yes / No), it _____.

5 Is it a cooker?
(Yes / No), it _____.

6 Is it a jumper?
(Yes / No), it _____.

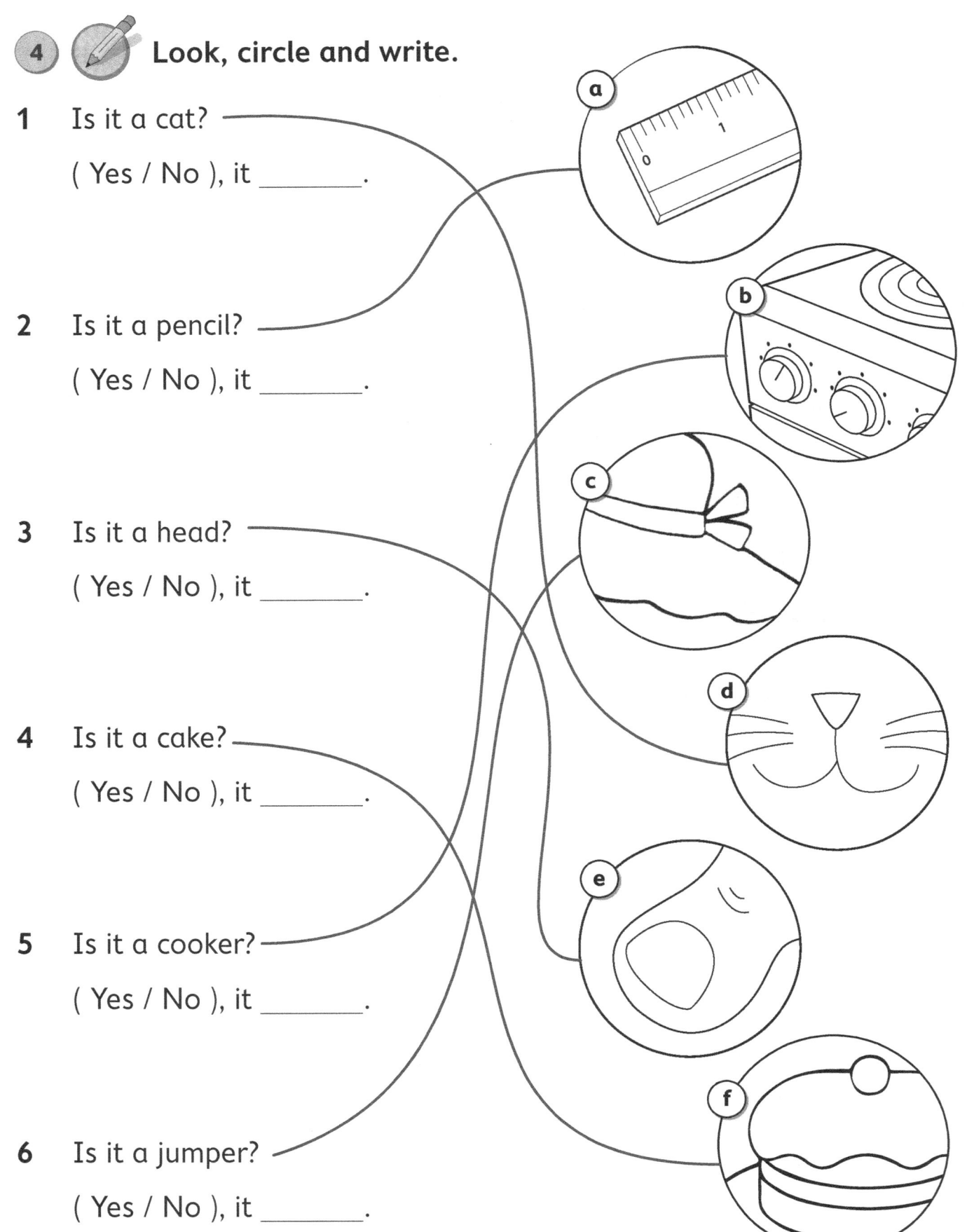

Lesson 3

5. Find and circle the odd words out. Then write.

1. cheese, (ruler), meat, salad — ruler
2. pencil, book, cat, rubber — _____
3. mum, dad, dancer, sister — _____
4. dog, shoes, rabbit, mouse — _____
5. artist, brother, farmer, teacher — _____
6. yoghurt, trousers, T-shirt, hat — _____
7. living room, kitchen, shop, bedroom — _____
8. park, bathroom, library, café — _____

6. Read and answer.

1. What's your favourite colour? _____.
2. What's your favourite animal? _____.
3. What's your favourite food? _____.
4. Who's your favourite character? _____.

Lesson 4

Halloween

1. ✏️ Match. Then trace.

witch   *pumpkin*   *cat*   *monster*   *bat*

2. ✏️ Join the dots. Then circle.

I'm a (monster / pumpkin / witch).

Christmas

1 Trace and match. Then listen and colour.

a) sleigh b) present c) reindeer d) Santa

2 Draw and say. Then read and trace.

To _____,
Happy
Christmas!
From Santa.

Easter

1   **Colour and write.**   chick   egg   ~~bunny~~

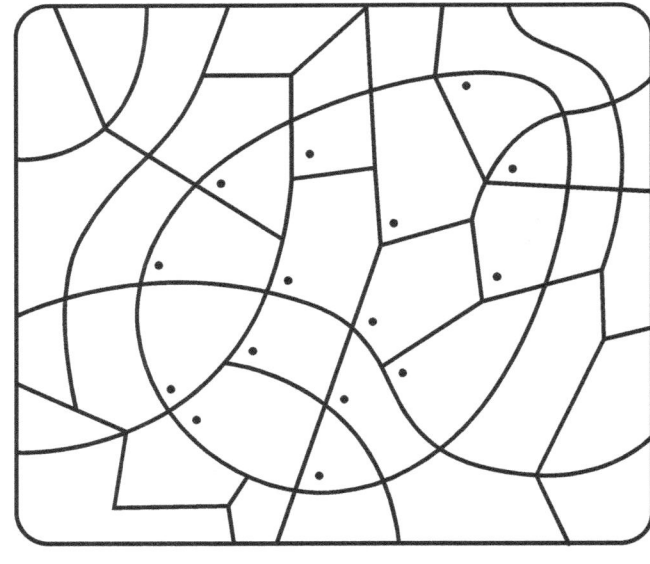

 bunny

 _____

 _____

It's an _____.

2 **Look and draw.**

   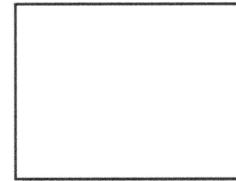

94 Easter

Summer fun

1 Read and match.

① sun ② sky ③ tree

④ bird ⑤ flower ⑥ grass

2 Choose and write. Then colour the picture in Activity 1.

~~blue~~ brown purple yellow green red

The sky is __blue__. The sun is _____.

The tree is _____. The bird is _____.

The flowers are _____. The grass is _____.

Summer fun

1 Extra practice

1 Choose and write.

My   Yes   ~~Hello~~   I'm   it
Her   you   your   is

a Hello. What's your name? — _____ name's Ellie.

b _____ name's Grace.

c How old are _____? — _____ four.

d What's _____ favourite colour? — My favourite colour _____ blue.

e What's your favourite colour? Is _____ blue? — _____, it is.

1  **Choose and write.**

> it   these   ~~this~~   blue
> pencils   They're   many
> they   book   Three

a What's _this_?   It's a _____.

b Is _____ red?   No, it isn't. It's blue. It's a _____ book.

c What are _____?   They're _____.

d What colour are _____?   _____ purple.

e How _____ pencils can you see?   _____.

Unit 2 Extra practice

3

1 Choose and write.

> this   Is   ~~He's~~   She's
> my   No   she

a This is my brother. __He's__ ten.

b And _____ is my sister.

How old is _____?

c _____ five.

d This is _____ mum.

_____ she a dentist?

e _____, she isn't. She's a vet.

Unit 3 Extra practice

1 Choose and write.

| He's   I've   ~~got~~   They're |

a)  He's _got_ a blue head and a red body.

b)  _____ got four arms. They're green.

c)  He's got three legs. _____ blue.

d)  _____ got a red head and a green body. I've got blue feet.

5

1 Choose and write.

> are   It's   They're   long   you
> Has   ~~What's~~   hasn't   I've

a) __What's__ that?   _____ a big cat.

b) What _____ those?   _____ rats.

c) _____ she got a rat?   No, she _____. She's got a hamster.

d) Have _____ got a rat?   No, I haven't. _____ got a snake.

It's a _____ snake!

Unit 5 Extra practice

1 Choose and write.

> are   Where's   under   There's
> She's   Theyre   ~~Where~~

a
Where are Mum and Dad?
_____ in the living room.

b
Where's Grace?
_____ in the bedroom.

c
Hmm. _____ a lamp on the desk.
There _____ two rabbits on the bed.

_____ Grace?

d
She's _____ the bed.

Unit 6 Extra practice

7

1 Choose and write.

Yes Thank ~~like~~ don't Do you

a) I __like__ sandwiches and fruit.
I _____ like meat.

b) _____ you like meat, Grace?
_____, I do. I like meat. I don't like sandwiches! 

c) Here _____ are.

d) _____ you!

Unit 7 Extra practice

1 Choose and write.

Are you they ~~I'm~~ am He's he Thank

a. I'm thirsty. — And __I'm__ hungry.

b. Are _____ hungry? — Yes, I _____

c. Is _____ hungry? — No, he isn't. _____ thirsty.

d. Here you are. — _____ you.

e. _____ they happy? — Yes, _____ are.

Unit 8 Extra practice

Unit 1

 **My birthday**

red yellow green blue pink purple orange brown black white grey

 **Numbers**

one two three four five six seven eight nine ten

 **Actions**

jump walk stamp clap run dance climb hop

 **Natural science**

bird fish flower leaf butterfly

Unit 2

 Classroom objects

 chair

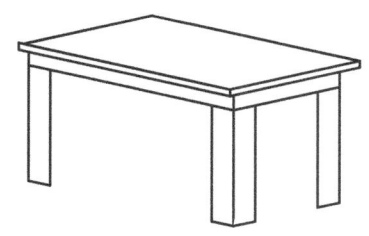 table

 pencil

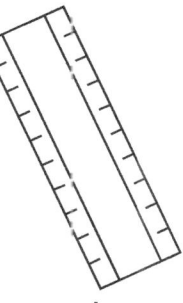 ruler

 pen

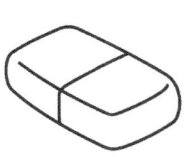 rubber

 book

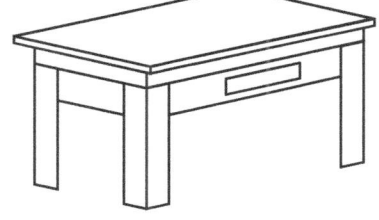 desk

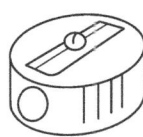 pencil sharpener

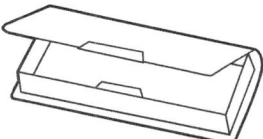 pencil case

 Numbers

 eleven

 twelve

 thirteen

 fourteen

 fifteen

 sixteen

 seventeen

 eighteen

 nineteen

 twenty

 Music

 guitar

 piano

 violin

 drum

Picture dictionary

Unit 3

 **My family**

mum   dad   brother   sister   friend   granny   grandad   aunt

 **Occupations**

   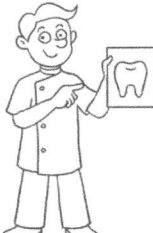

doctor   cook   vet   dentist

pilot   artist   dancer   farmer   teacher

 **Art**

 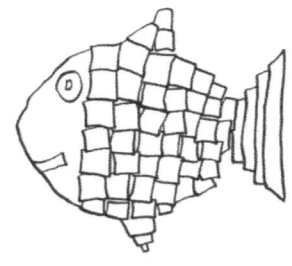  

painting   collage   drawing   sculpture

Unit 4
My body

 head
 arms
 feet
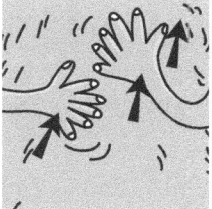 hands
 body

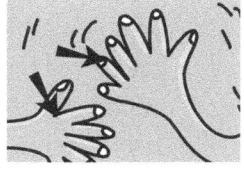 fingers
 legs
 toes
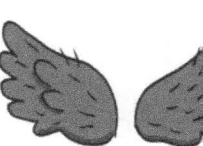 wings
 tail

 Clothes

 T-shirt
 jumper
 trousers
 dress

 skirt
 shoes
 socks
 hat

 Natural Science

 clean hands
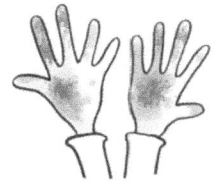 dirty hands
 a dirty face
 wash your hands

Unit 5

Pets

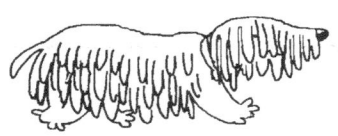 dog

 cat

 rabbit

 parrot

 mouse

 tortoise

 frog

 snake

 hamster

Adjectives

 big

 small

 tall

 short

 long

 thin

 fat

 young

 old

Natural science

 chick

 kitten

 puppy

 egg

 goose

 bird

Unit 6

 ## At home (1)

kitchen	living room	door	garden
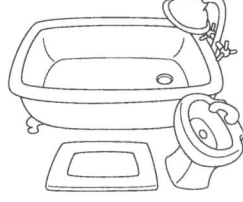		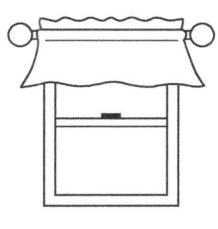	
bathroom	bedroom	window	house

 ## At home (2)

	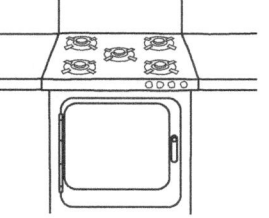	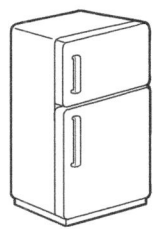	
bath	cooker	fridge	TV
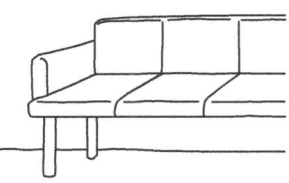	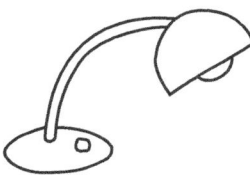		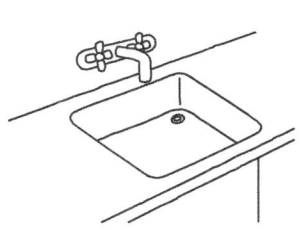
sofa	lamp	bed	sink

 ## Social Science

shop	library	playground	café	park

Unit 7

 ## Food (1)

 cake
 fruit
 bread
 cheese
 fish

 yoghurt
 milk
 juice
 salad

 ## Food (2)

 sandwich
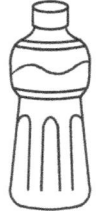 water
 chocolate
 honey

 jelly
 vegetables
 ice cream
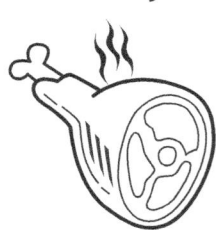 meat

 ## Natural science

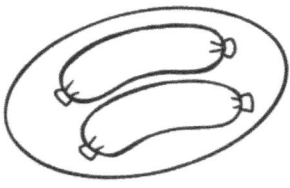 sausages
 chips
 carrots

Picture dictionary

Unit 8
Adjectives (1)

happy   scared   tired   hungry   thirsty

Adjectives (2)

sad   hot   cold   ill   hurt   angry   bored

 Natural science

It's hot.   It's cold.

Picture dictionary

Pearson Education Limited
Edinburgh Gate
Harlow
Essex CM20 2JE
England
and Associated Companies throughout the world.

Poptropica® English Islands

© Pearson Education Limited 2017

Editorial and project management by hyphen

All rights reserved; no part of this publication may be reproduced, stored in a retrieval system, or transmitted in any form or by any means, electronic, mechanical, photocopying, recording, or otherwise without the prior written permission of the Publishers.

First published 2017
ISBN: 978-1-2921-9808-8

Set in Fiendstar 17/21pt

Acknowledgements: The publisher would like to thank Tessa Lochowski, Steve Elsworth and Jim Rose for their contributions to this edition.

Illustrators: Chan Siu Fai, Moreno Chiacchiera (Beehive Illustration), Adam Clay, Leo Cultura, Andrew Hennessey, James Horvath (Beehive Illustration), Marek Jagucki, Sue King, Stephenine Lau, Daniel Limon (Beehive Illustration), Katie McDee, Bill McGuire (Shannon Associates), Jackie Stafford, Olimpia Wong and Yam Wai Lun

Picture Credits: The publisher would like to thank the following for their kind permission to reproduce their photographs:
(Key: b-bottom; c-centre; l-left; r-right; t-top)

Shutterstock.com: forden 85l, Svitlana-ua 85r

Cover images: *Back:* **Fotolia.com:** frender r; **Shutterstock.com:** Denys Prykhodov l

All other images © Pearson Education

Every effort has been made to trace the copyright holders and we apologize in advance for any unintentional omissions. We would be pleased to insert the appropriate acknowledgement in any subsequent edition of this publication.